E S T A T E   P U B

G000038588

ROYAL TUNBRIDG
TONBRIDGE SOUTHB___

CROWBOROUGH · EDENBRIDGE etc.

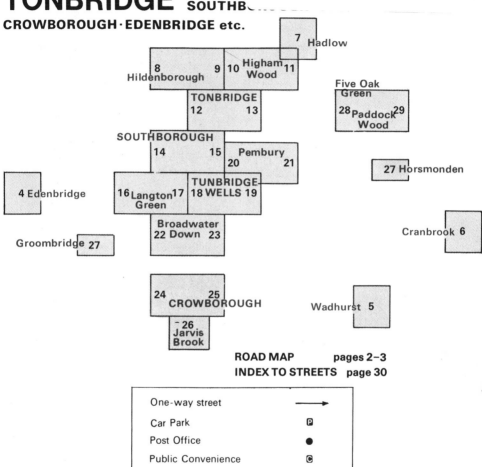

	7 Hadlow	
8	9	10 Higham 11 Wood
Hildenborough		
	Five Oak Green	
TONBRIDGE	28 Paddock 29 Wood	
12	13	
SOUTHBOROUGH		
14	15 Pembury	27 Horsmonden
	20 21	
4 Edenbridge	TUNBRIDGE	
16 Langton 17 18 WELLS 19		
Green	Cranbrook 6	
Broadwater		
Groombridge 27	22 Down 23	
24 25 CROWBOROUGH	Wadhurst 5	
- 26 Jarvis Brook		

ROAD MAP   pages 2–3
INDEX TO STREETS   page 30

One-way street	→
Car Park	🄿
Post Office	●
Public Convenience	🄲
Place of worship	+
Scale of street plans: 4 inches to 1 mile	

Street plans prepared and published by ESTATE PUBLICATIONS, Bridewell House, Tenterden, Kent and based upon the ORDNANCE SURVEY maps with the sanction of the controller of H.M. Stationery Office.

The publishers acknowledge the co-operation of Tunbridge Wells Wealden, and Tonbridge & Malling District Councils in the preparation of these maps.

0 86084 330 0

ROAD MAP

2

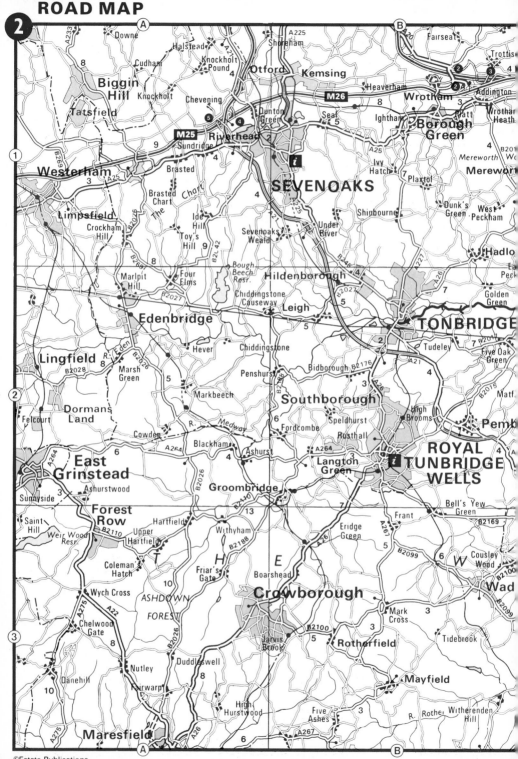

©Estate Publications

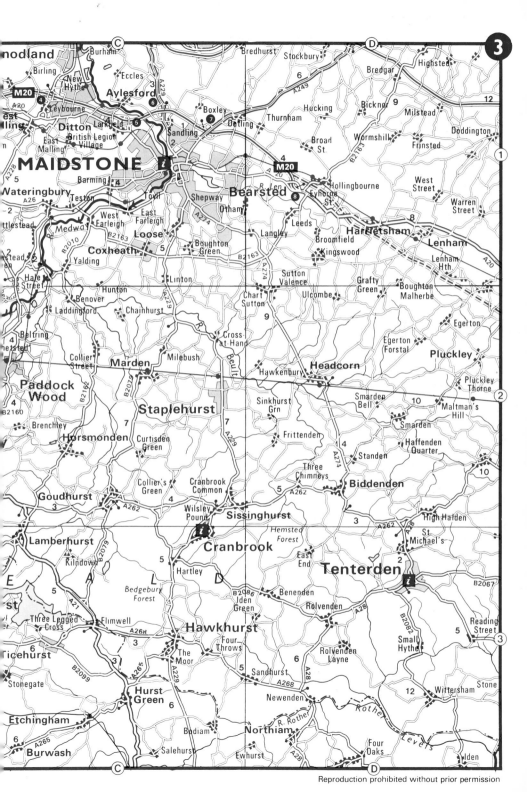

3

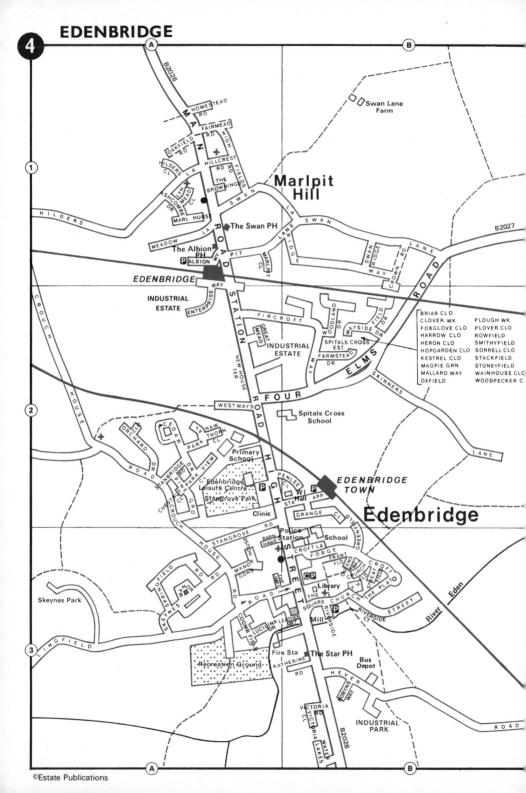

Marlpit Hill

Edenbridge

EDENBRIDGE TOWN

The Swan PH

The Albion PH

Swan Lane Farm

INDUSTRIAL ESTATE

INDUSTRIAL ESTATE

Spitals Cross School

Spitals Cross Est

Primary School

Edenbridge Leisure Centre

Stangrove Park

Clinic

Police Station

School

Library

Skeynes Park

Recreation Ground

Fire Sta

The Star PH

Bus Depot

INDUSTRIAL PARK

Water Lakes

BRIAR CLO
CLOVER WK
FOXGLOVE CLO
HARROW CLO
HERON CLO
HOPGARDEN CLO
KESTREL CLO
MAGPIE GRN
MALLARD WAY
OXFIELD

PLOUGH WK
PLOVER CLO
ROWFIELD
SMITHYFIELD
SORRELL CLO
STACKFIELD
STONEYFIELD
WAINHOUSE CLO
WOODPECKER C

River Eden

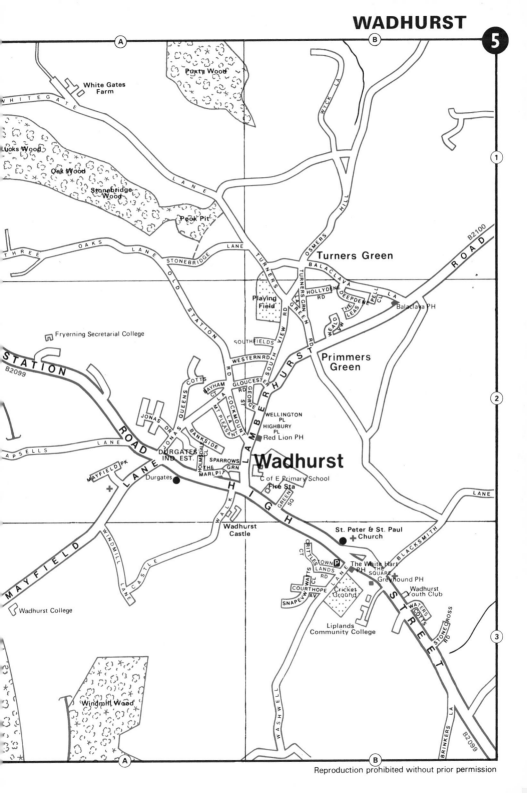

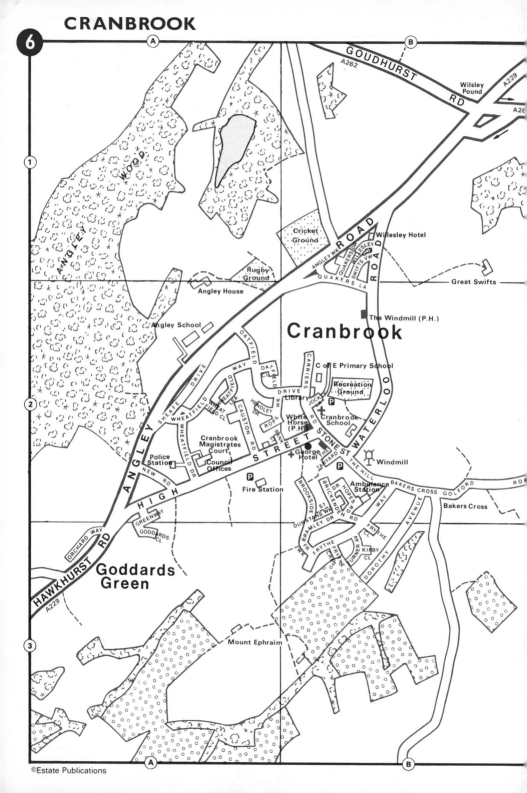

Cranbrook

Goddards Green

GOUDHURST RD
A262
Wilsley Pound
A229
A26

WOOD

ANGLEY

Cricket Ground

Wilsley Hotel

Great Swifts

The Windmill (P.H.)

Rugby Ground

Angley House

Angley School

ANGLEY WAY
QUAKERS DR
WILSLEY DR
SWIFTS VW
QUAKERS LA

ROAD

C of E Primary School

CARRIERS
OATFIELD WAY
OATFIELD
OATFIELD WK
DRIVE
Library
JOCKS
Recreation Ground

Cranbrook School

SHEAFE DRIVE
WHEATFIELD DRIVE
WHEATFIELD CL
CAUSTON RD
HENDLEY DR
ROPE LANE

WHEAT CL

White Horse (P.H.)

Cranbrook Magistrates Court

Police Station

Council Offices

NEW RD

George Hotel

STONE ST

STREET

HIGH

Fire Station

THE HILL
Windmill

Ambulance Station

BAKERS CROSS
GOLFORD RD

Bakers Cross

WATERLOO

THE WAY

IANYARD

BRICKENDEN RD
HOPES RD

BROOKSIDE

DUNSTANS WK
BRAMLEY DR
ST DUNSTANS
ERYTHE CRES
FRYTHE WK
FRYTHE CL
KIRBY CL
TURNER AV
DOROTHY
AVENUE
FRYTHE CL

GREENWAY
GODDARDS CL

ORCHARD WAY

HAWKHURST RD
A229

Mount Ephraim

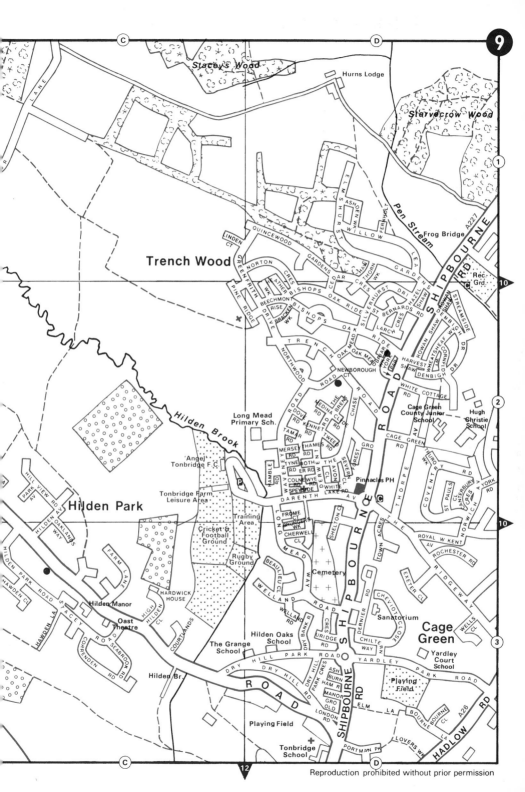

Stacey's Wood

Hurns Lodge

Starvecrow Wood

Pen Stream

Frog Bridge

A227

SHIPBOURNE RD

Rec Grd

Trench Wood

LINDEN CT

QUINCEWOOD GARDENS

ELMSHURST

ASHON

WILLOW

FERNHURST

LEADEN

GARDENS

NORTON CRES

GREENRITH

PINE RIDGE

FEATHER WK

BEECHMONT

RISE

BISHOPS RISE

BRACKEN WK

DRIVE

BISHOPS

OAK

OAK RIDE

DEER CRES

SILVERHURST DR

LARCH CRES

THORN WK

BERNARDS RD

HAZEL SHAW

HOWAN SHAW

WHEATSHEAF SHAW

DENBIGH

CORNFORD

NBIGH DR

STREAMSIDE

Trench Wood

NORTHWOOD

TRENCH

OAK

OAK MEAD

OAK RIDE

THE BRENT

ROAD

ROAD

CHASE

HARVEST SHAW

DENBIGH RD

WHITE COTTAGE

NEWBOROUGH CT

Long Mead Primary Sch.

RODVE RD

MEDINA CL

KENNET RD

TWEED

SEVERN RD

FOREST GRO

CAGE GREEN RD

Cage Green County Junior School

Hugh Christie School

Hilden Brook

TAMAR RD

MERSEY RD

THAMES RD

ROTHER RD

DERWENT

THE AVON

THORPE

COVENTRY WK

ST PAULS

CANTERBURY CRES

NORWICH RD

YORK RD

'Angel' Tonbridge F.C.

TYNE RD

COLNE

WYE

SPEYSIDE

WHITE LAKE AV

Pinnacles PH

Tonbridge Farm Leisure Area

HAMBLE

WAVENEY

DARENTH

Training Area

FROME CT

BRUNTERS WK

CHERWELL CL

SHELTON CL

TOWN ACRES

RIDGEWAY

ROYAL W KENT AV

ROCHESTER RD

Cricket & Football Ground

MEAD

Cemetery

DERNIER RD

CHEVIOT CL

EXETER CL

Hilden Park

PARK VIEW AV

HILDEN PARK ROAD

OAKLANDS WAY

FARM LANE

Rugby Ground

WELLAND ROAD

Sanatorium

Cage Green

WELLS CL

HAWDEN CL

HILDEN PARK ROAD

STACEY ROAD

HIGH HILDEN CL

COURTLANDS

HARDWICK HOUSE

Hilden Manor

Oast Theatre

BEAULIEU CL

WELLAND CRES

URIDGE RD

CHILTERN WAY

Yardley Court School

HAWDEN LA

SEABROOK RD

CORRENDEN RD

The Grange School

Hilden Oaks School

BANK R

MANOR RD

OLD RD

ASH BURN

HAM R

DRY HILL PARK CRES

Playing Field

Hilden Br.

DRY HILL ROAD

DRY HILL PARK ROAD

SHIPBOURNE RD

ELM LA

BOURNE CL

BOURNE RD

A26

HADLOW RD

LONDON RD

LOVERS WK

Playing Field

Tonbridge School

PORTMAN PK

YARDLEY ROAD

1

10

2

10

3

C   D

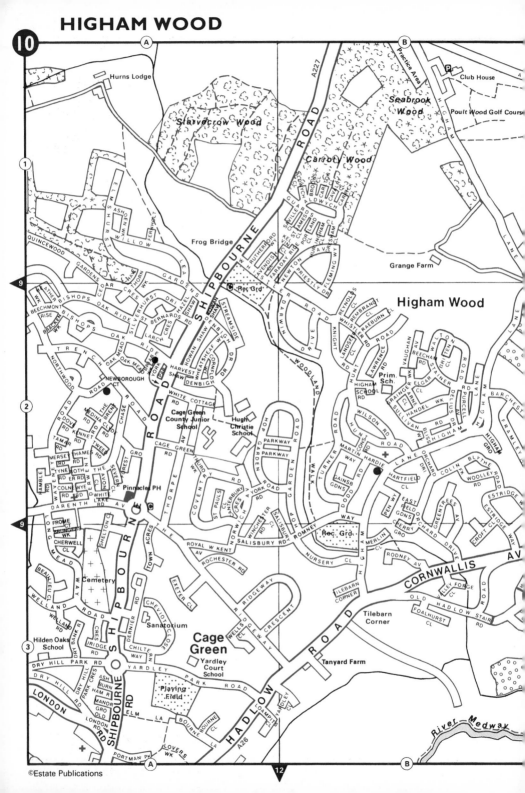

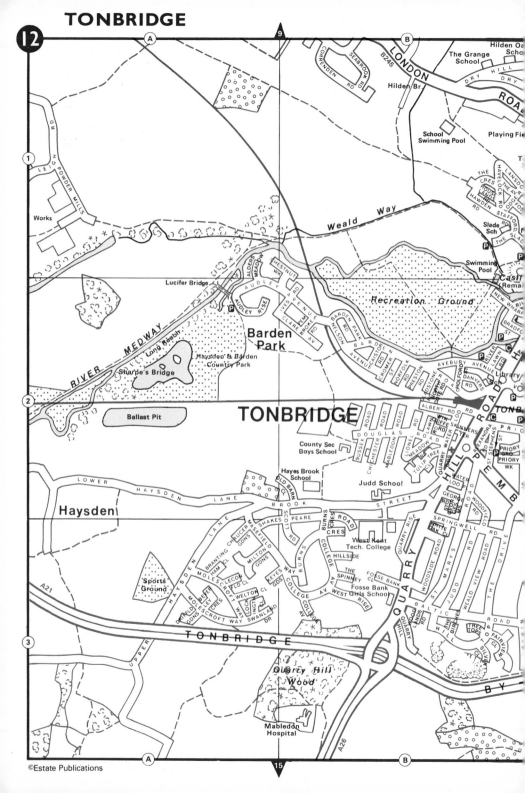

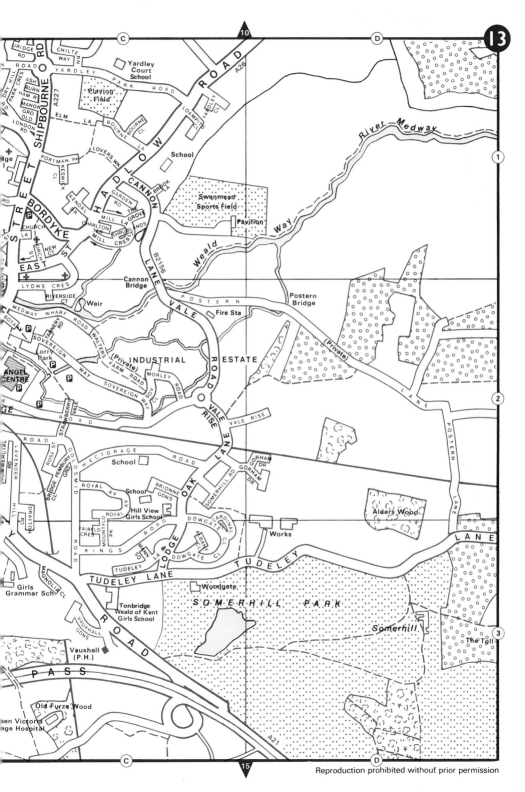

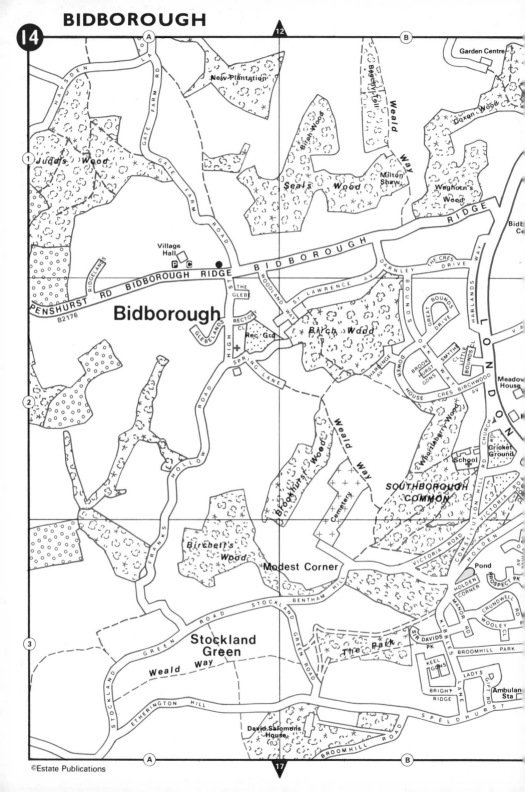

Bidborough

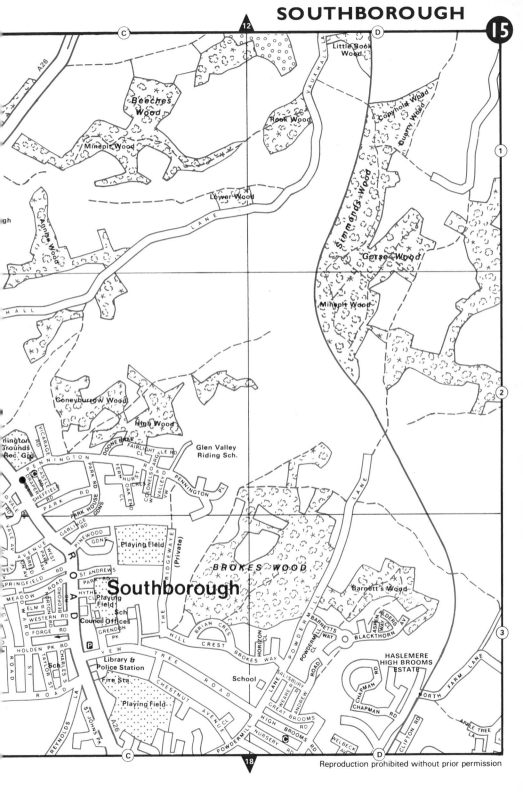

Speldhurst

Weald Way

Langton
Green

The Greyhound
PH

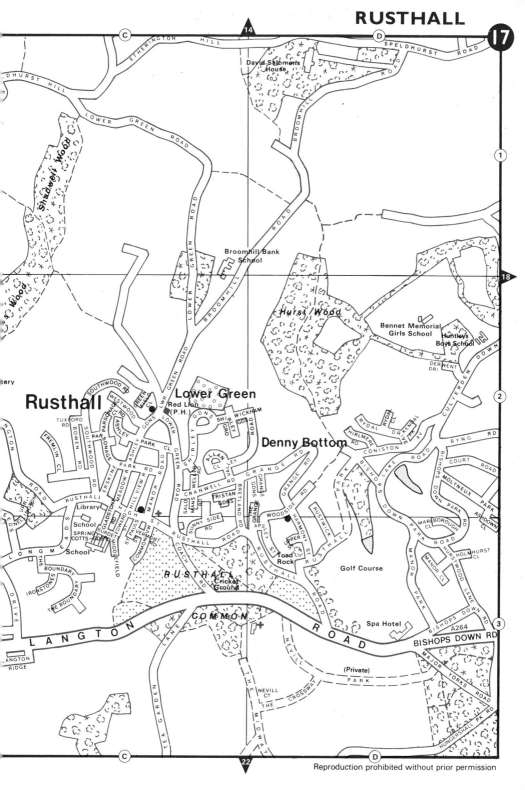

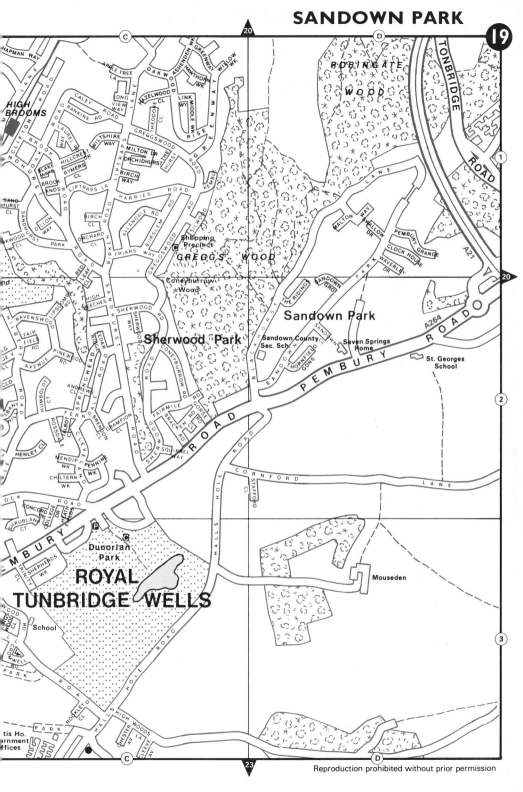

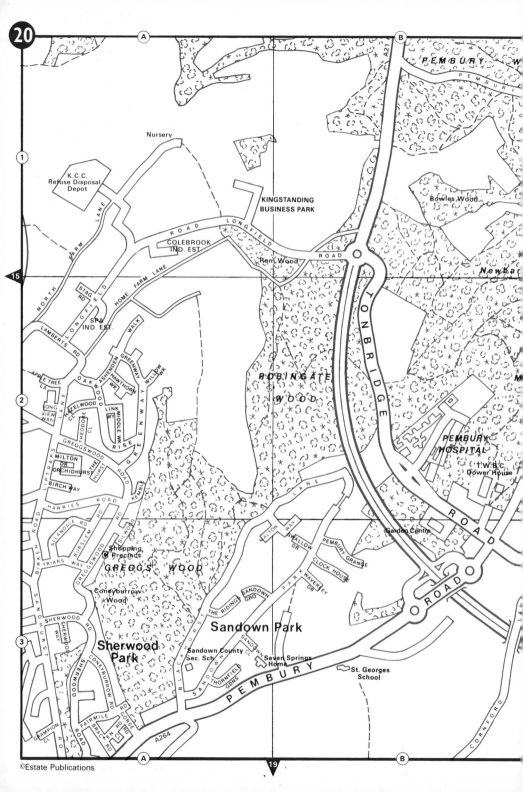

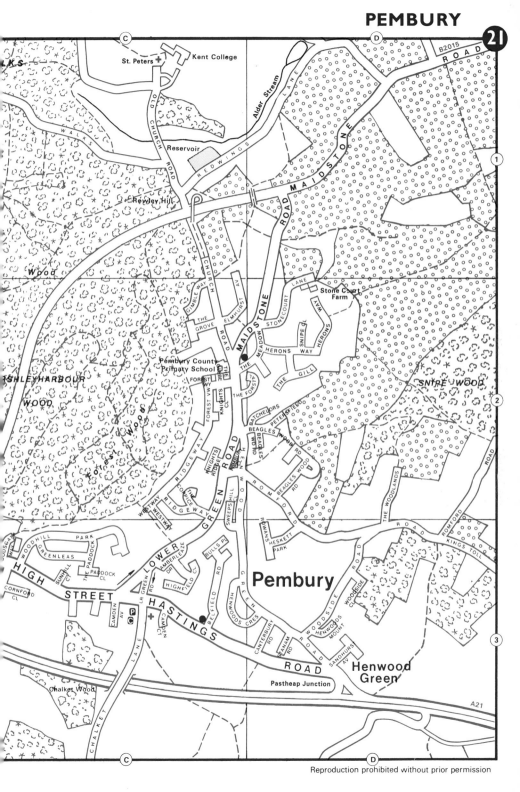

Pembury

Henwood Green

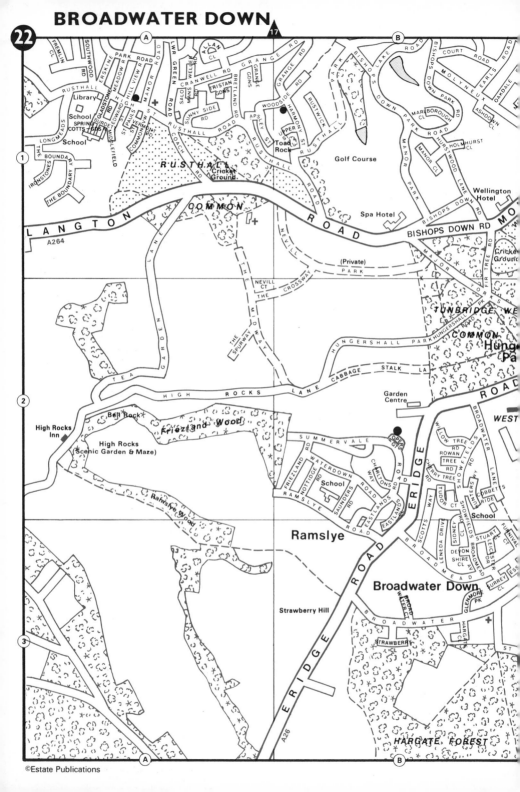

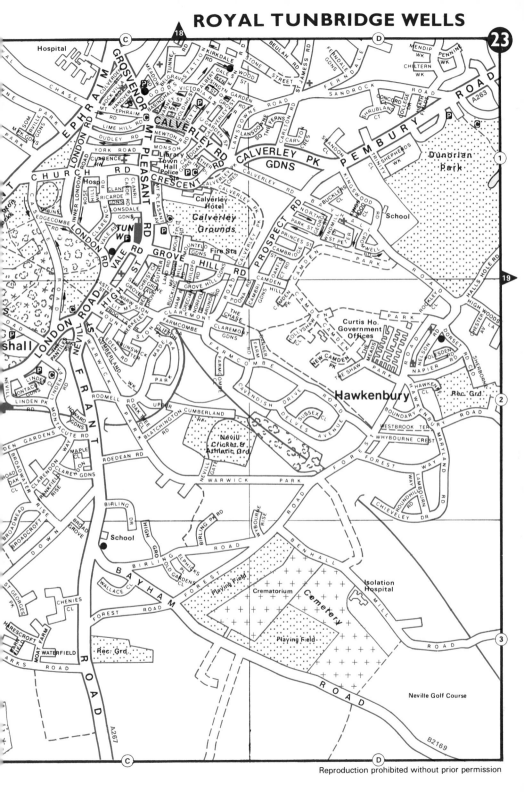

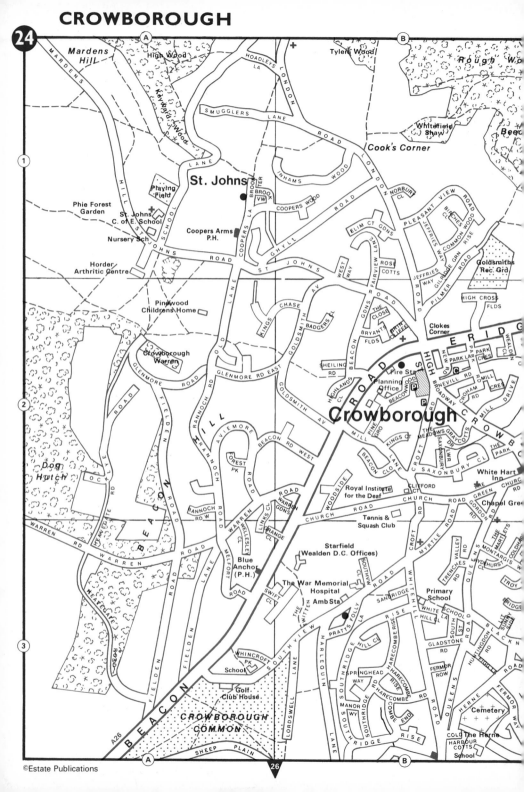

A
B

1

2

3

26

Mardens Hill
High Wood
Tylers Wood
Rough Wo
HOADLEYS LA
LONDON ROAD
Whitefield Shaw
Beec
Cook's Corner
SMUGGLERS LANE
Keysford Wood
HILL
MARDENS
INHAMS WOOD
ROAD
Phie Forest Garden
Playing Field
St. Johns
BROOK
BROOK VW
COOPERS WOOD
NORBURY CL
PLEASANT VIEW
BIRCHES
COMMON WOOD
ROAD
St. Johns C. of E. School
Nursery Sch
COOPERS LA
SCHOOL
LANE
Coopers Arms P.H.
COOPERS
ST. JOHNS
GHYLL
ROAD
ELIM CT GDNS
WEST WAY
FAIRVIEW LANE
ROSE COTTS
JEFFRIES WAY
GILRIDGE GRN
PILMER
RISE
ROAD
Goldsmiths Rec. Grd
Horder Arthritic Centre
ROAD
JEFFRIES
High Cross Flds
Pinewood Childrens Home
KINGS
CHASE
GOLDSMITH AV
BADGERS F
GDNS
THE CLOSE
BRYANTS FLDS
Clokes Corner
ERIDGE
HIGH CROSS FLDS
Crowborough Warren
OLD
LANE
GLENMORE RD EAST
SHEILING RD
BEACON
HIGHLANDS RD
Fire Sta
NEW ROW
PARK LA
PARK CRES
WEALDEN
GROSS
GLENMORE ROAD
RANNOCH HILL
AVIEMORE ROAD
Planning Office
BEACON
BROADWAY
GOHAM RD
MILL CRES
DRIVE
HIGH ST
ROAD
CROW BO
Dog Hatch
FIELDEN
ROAD
BEACON
CREST PK
BEACON RD WEST
MILL LANE
PINE GRO
KINGS CT
CROFT
SAXONBURY
SAXONBURY CL
GRAYCOTTS
THE MEADOWS
THE PARK
Crowborough
ROAD
RANNOCH ROAD
RANNOCH RD. W
WARREN GDNS
WELLESLEY CL
GRANGE CL
LINKS CL
MELFORT RD
Royal Institute for the Deaf
WOODSIDE
CLIFFORD CT
White Hart Inn
CHURCH
Chapel Gree
THE MARTLETS
COLOMB
MONTARGIS
HYDEHURST CL
TROY
BEACON
WARREN RD
HEATHGATE
FIELDEN LANE
ROAD
Blue Anchor (P.H.)
SWIFT CL
Starfield (Wealden D.C. Offices)
CHURCH ROAD
ROAD
Tennis & Squash Club
CROFT RD
MYRTLE ROAD
GORDON RD
QUEENS
TRENCHES RD
ANTHOR
The War Memorial Hospital
Amb Sta
SANDRIDGE
SOUTHVIEW
WHITEHILL
Primary School
WHITE HILL CL
SCHOOL
GLADSTONE RD
FERMOR ROW
HUNTINGDON RD
BIGGS
WARREN RD
SOUTH VIEW
THE WITTEN
PRATTS FOLLY LA
HARLEQUIN
HILL CL
HARECOMBE RISE
RISE
SPRINGHEAD WAY
HARECOMBE RISE
HARECOMBE RD
SOUTH RD
ST
QUEENS ROAD
HERNE
FERMOR WAY
Cemetery
WHINCROFT PK
School
LORDSWELL LANE
SOUTHRIDGE
MANOR WY
SOUTHRIDGE
HARECOMBE END
RISE
COLD HARBOUR COTTS
The Herne
School
Golf Club House
CROWBOROUGH COMMON
A26
BEACON
ROAD
SHEEP PLAIN

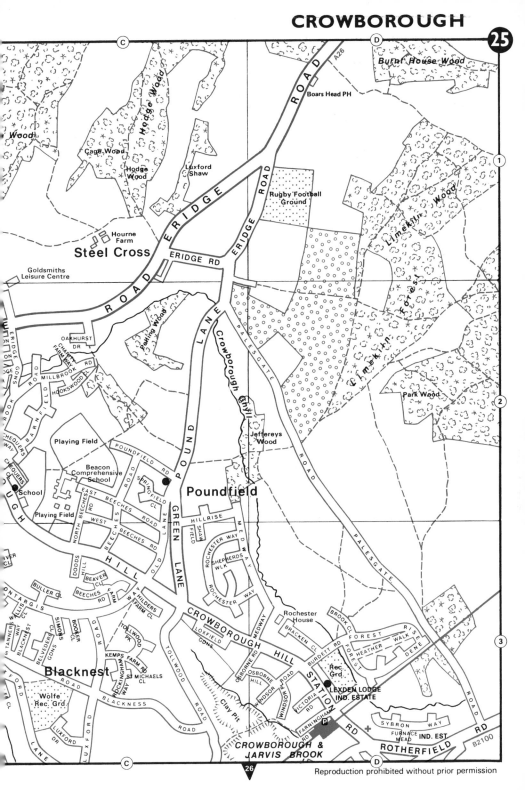

CROWBOROUGH

Burnt House Wood

A26

Boars Head PH

ERIDGE ROAD

Wood

Cage Wood

Hodge Wood

Hodge Wood

Luxford Shaw

Rugby Football Ground

Limekiln Wood

Hourne Farm

Steel Cross

ERIDGE RD

Forest

Goldsmiths Leisure Centre

ERIDGE ROAD

Park Wood

OAKHURST DR

Peeling Wood

PALESGATE

CHARTWELL

CHART FARM WALK

MILLBROOK CL

HOOKSWOOD RD

POUND LANE

Crowborough Ghyll

Jeffereys Wood

BARNFIELD ROAD

CHEQUERS WAY

Playing Field

POUNDFIELD RD

Beacon Comprehensive School

SPRINGFIELD CL

Poundfield

School

EAST BEECHES RD

POUND LANE

OLD LANE

GREEN LANE

Playing Field

NORTH BEECHES

WEST BEECHES

BEECHES ROAD

HILLRISE

SHAW FIELD

MEDWAY

PALESGATE

HILL

DODDS HILL

BEAVER CL

ROCHESTER WAY

SHEPHERDS WLK

BULLER CL

BEECHES RD

FARM

HILDERS FARM CL

ROCHESTER WAY

Rochester House

BRACKEN CL

BROOK CL

FOREST RISE

ONTARGIS WAY

ST TANNERS WILLIS WAY

SIMONS CL

BOOKER CL

ROAD

TOLLWOOD PK

W 4

CROWBOROUGH HILL

MEDWAY

HEATHER WALK

DENE

BLACKNEST

BELVEDERE GDNS

KEMPS FARM RD

ROCKINGHAM WAY

ST MICHAELS CL

TOLLWOOD ROAD

LOXFIELD GDNS

OSBORNE RD

OSBORNE HILL

WINDSOR ROAD

BURDETT RD

Rec Grd.

FOREST ROAD

Blacknest

Wolfe Rec. Grd.

ROAD

BLACKNESS ROAD

LUXFORD DR

LANE

Clay Pit

VICTORIA RD

STATION RD

FARNINGHAM RD

P

LEXDEN LODGE IND. ESTATE

SYBRON WAY

FURNACE MEAD IND. EST

ROTHERFIELD RD

B2100

CROWBOROUGH & JARVIS BROOK

Reproduction prohibited without prior permission

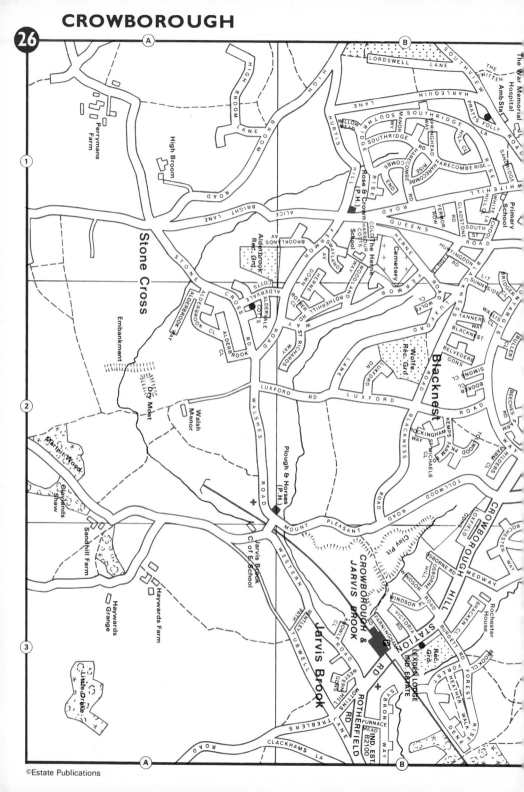

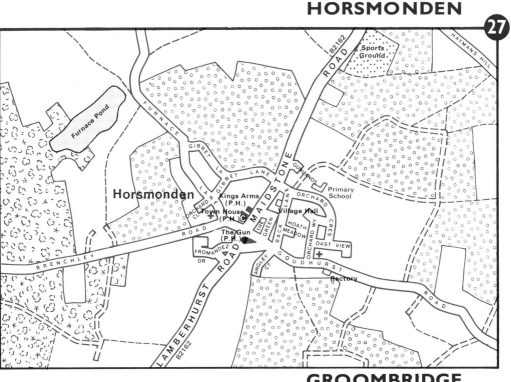

GROOMBRIDGE

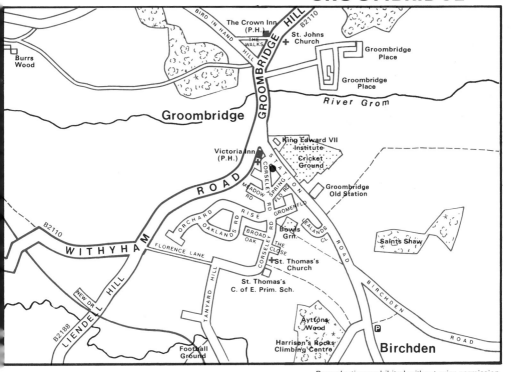

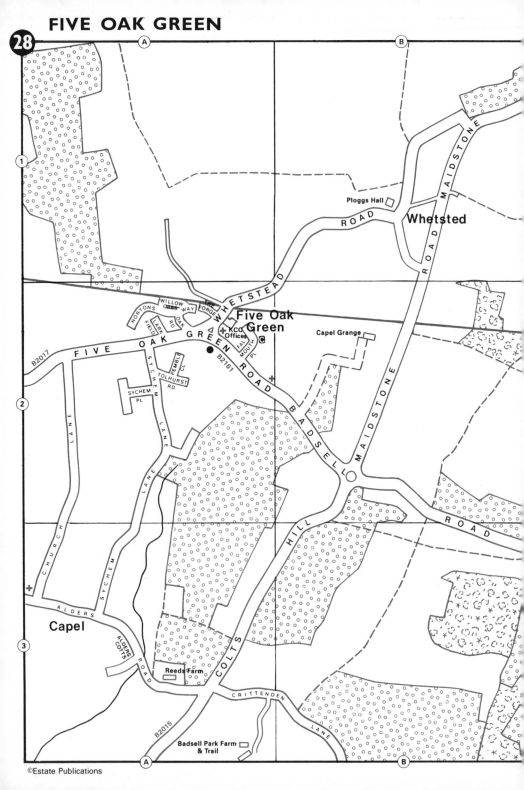

Whetsted

Ploggs Hall

Five Oak Green

Capel Grange

KCO Offices

WILLOW WAY

The Forge

MORTONS

OAK RD

LARK FIELD

PEMBLE CL

TOLHURST RD

SYCHEM PL

SYCHEM LANE

B2017

FIVE OAK GREEN ROAD

B2161

BADSELL ROAD

MAIDSTONE ROAD

MAIDSTONE ROAD

WHETSTEAD

HILL

FALMOUTH PL

CHURCH LANE

SYCHEM LANE

ALDERS

ALDERS COTTS

Capel

Reeds Farm

COLTS ROAD

COLTS LANE

CRITTENDEN LANE

B2015

Badsell Park Farm & Trail

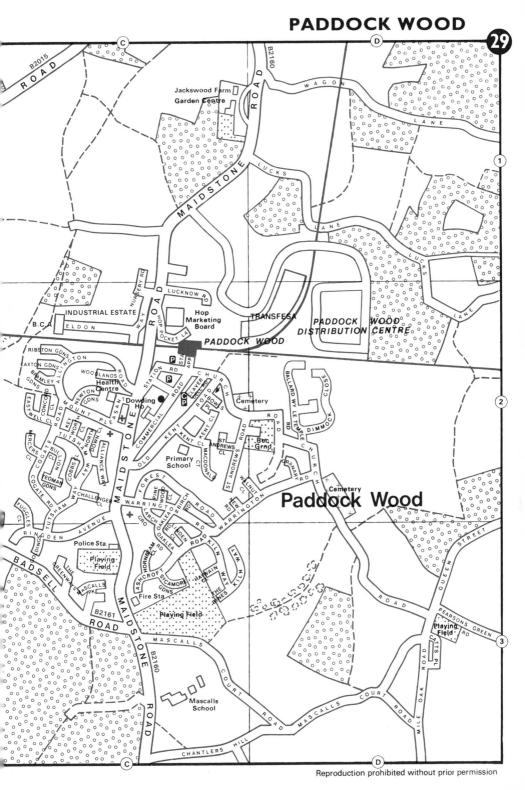

Paddock Wood

INDEX TO STREETS

TONBRIDGE

Albany Clo 13 C3
Albert Rd 12 B2
Alders Meadow 12 A1
Aldwych 10 B1
Aldwych Clo 10 B1
Alexandra Rd 12 B2
Allington Dri 11 C2
Angel La 12 B2
Appletons 7 B2
Arne Clo 10 B2
Ashburnham Rd 9 D3
Ashden Walk 9 D1
Ashes La 11 C1
Ashley Rd 8 B2
Audley Av 12 A2
Audley Rise 12 A2
Avebury Av 12 B2
Avon Clo 9 D2

Baltic Rd 12 B3
Bank St 13 C1
Barchester Way 10 B2
Barclay Av 11 C3
Barden Park Rd 12 B2
Barden Rd 12 B2
Beaulieu Clo 9 D3
Beecham Rd 10 B2
Beechmont Rise 9 D2
Bell Row 7 B3
Beverley Cres 12 A3
Birch Clo 8 B3
Bishops Oak Rise 9 D2
Blackmans La 7 A2
Bliss Way 10 B2
Bordyke 13 C1
Botany 13 C2
Bourne Clo 10 A3
Bourne Grange La 7 A2
Bourne La 10 A3
Bracken Walk 9 D2
Bradford St 12 B2
Bramble Clo 8 B3
Brantingham Clo 12 A3
Briar Walk 9 D2
Bridge Clo 13 C2
Brionne Gdns 13 C2
Britten Clo 10 B2
Broadway 7 A2
Brook La 13 C1
Brook St 12 B2
Brookfields 7 A2
Brookmead 8 B3
Brooks Clo 10 B1
Brungers Walk 9 D3
Burns Cres 12 B3
Byrneside 8 B3

Cage Green La 10 A2
Caistor Rd 12 B2
Cannon La 13 C1
Canterbury Cres 10 A2
Cardinal Clo 13 C3
Carlton Clo 10 B1
Carpenters La 7 A1
Carrick Clo 10 B1
Castle St 13 C1
Cavalry Clo 10 B1
Cavendish Clo 10 A1
Caxton La 7 A2
Cedar Cres 9 D1
Cemetary La 7 B2
Charlton Ter 13 C1
Chaucer Gdn 12 A3
Cherry Gro 10 B2
Cherwell Clo 9 D3
Chestnut Walk 12 B1
Cheviot Clo 10 A3
Chichester Rd 12 B2
Chiltern Way 10 A3
Church La 13 C1
Church Rd 8 B2
Church St 7 A2
Clare Av 12 B2
Clyde Rd 9 D2
Coldharbour La 8 B2
Colin Blythe Rd 10 B2
College Av 9 D2
Colne Rd 9 D2
Commercial Rd 13 C2
Constable Rd 10 B2
Copse Rd 8 B3
Cornfield Way 10 A2
Cornwallis Av 10 B3
Correnden Rd 9 C3
Court La 7 B2
Courtlands 9 C3
Coventry Rd 10 A2
Cranford Rd 11 C2
Croft Clo 10 B3
Cromer St 12 B2
Cuckoo La 11 C2

Danvers Rd 12 B2
Darenth Av 9 D2
Darwin Dri 10 B2
Deakin Leas 12 B3
Delius Dri 10 B2
Denbigh Dri 10 A2
Derby Clo 8 B2
Dernier Rd 10 A3
Derwent Rd 9 D2
Dodd La 10 B2
Douglas Rd 12 B2
Dove Rd 9 D2
Dowgate Clo 13 C3

Drayton Rd 13 C2
Driffield Gdns 12 A3
Dry Bank Rd 9 D3
Dry Hill Park Cres 9 D3
Dry Hill Park Rd 9 D3
Dry Hill Rd 9 D3

East St 13 C1
Eastfield Gdns 10 B2
Eigar Clo 10 B2
Elm Gro 8 B3
Elm La 9 D3
Elmshurst Gdns 9 D1
Estridge Way 10 B2
Exeter Clo 10 A3

Fairfield Cres 13 C3
Fairfield Way 8 B2
Fairview Clo 12 B3
Faraday Ride 10 A1
Farm La 9 C3
Fellowes Way 8 B2
Fernholt 9 D1
Fir Tree Lodge 8 B2
Fleming Way 10 B1
Foalhurst Clo 10 B3
Forest Gro 9 D2
Fosse Bank Clo 12 B3
Fosse Rd 12 B1
Foxbush 8 A1
Framley Rd 10 B2
Francis Rd 8 B2
Frank Woolley Rd 10 B2
Frome Ct 9 D2

Gainsborough Gdns 10 B2
Garden Rd 13 C1
Garlands 8 B1
George Rd 12 B2
Goldsmid Rd 13 C2
Gorham Dri 13 D2
Grainger Walk 10 B2
Great Elms 7 A1
Green Frith Dri 9 D2
Greentrees Av 10 B2
Greenview Cres 8 B3
Gresham Clo 10 B1
Guards Clo 10 B1
Guestwick 10 B2

Hadlow Park 7 B1
Hadlow Rd 10 A3
Hadlow Stair 10 A3
Half Moon La 8 B2
Hamble Rd 9 D2
Handel Walk 10 B2
Hardwick House 9 C3
Hardwick Rd 8 B1
Hartfield Clo 10 B2
Hartlake La 11 D3
Harvest Shaw 10 A2
Havelock Rd 12 B1
Hawden Clo 9 C3
Hawden La 9 C3
Hawden Rd 12 B1
Hawthorn Walk 9 D1
Hazelshaw 9 D2
Heather Walk 9 D2
Hectorage Rd 13 C2
High Hilden Clo 9 C3
High House La 11 C1
High St, Hadlow 7 A2
High St, Tonbridge 13 C2
Higham Gdns 10 B2
Higham La 10 B1
Higham School Rd 10 B2
Hilden Av 9 C2
Hilden Park Rd 9 C3
Hill Top 12 B3
Hill View Rd 9 C2
Hillside 12 B3
Holford St 12 B2
Hop Garden Rd 10 A2
Hope Av 7 A1
Houselands Rd 12 B1
Hunt Rd 10 B2
Hurlingham Clo 10 B1

INDUSTRIAL ESTATES:
Sovereign Way
Ind. Est. 13 C2
Ives Rd 12 B2

Judd Rd 12 B3

Kelchers La 7 B3
Kelvin Clo 10 B1
Kendal Dri 13 C1
Kennet Rd 9 D2
Kenward Rd 7 A2
Keswick Clo 13 C1
Keyes Gdns 12 A3
Kings Rd 13 C3
Knight Rd 10 B2
Knowsley Way 8 B2

Landseer Clo 10 B2
Lansdowne Rd 12 B1
Larch Clo 10 B2
Lavender Hill 13 C2
Lawn Rd 12 B2
Lawrence Rd 10 B2
Leconfield Clo 12 A3
Leeds House Mews 7 A2
Leigh Rd 8 B2
Leybank 8 B3
Linden Ct 9 C1

Lionel Rd 12 B2
Loampits Clo 10 A3
Lockington Clo 12 B3
Lodge Oak La 13 C2
Lodge Rd 12 B1
London Rd 8 A1
Lonewood Way 7 B1
Long Mead Way 9 D3
Lovers Walk 9 D3
Lower Hayesden La 12 A2
Lyons Cres 13 C2

Mabledon Rd 12 B2
Magnolia Clo 13 C3
Maidstone Rd 7 B1
Maltings Clo 7 A2
Mann Sq 13 C3
Manor Gro 9 D3
Marshall Gdns 7 A1
Martin Hardie Way 10 B3
Masefield Way 12 A3
Meadow Rd 12 B2
Meadway 8 B2
Medina Rd 9 D2
Medway View 7 B3
Medway Wharf Rd 13 C2
Merlin Clo 10 B3
Mersey Rd 9 D2
Mill Cres 13 C1
Mill La, Hildenborough 8 A1
Mill La, Tonbridge 13 C1
Milton Gdns 12 A3
Molescroft Way 12 A3
Morley Rd 13 C2
Mount Pleasant 8 B2
Mount Pleasant Ct 8 B2
Mountfield Park 13 C3

Nelson Av 12 B2
New Ct 13 C1
New Wharf Rd 12 B2
Newborough Ct 9 D2
Newton Av 10 B1
Noble Rd 8 A2
Norfolk Rd 12 B2
Northcote Rd 12 B2
Northwood Rd 9 D2
Norton Cres 9 D1
Norwich Av 10 A3
Nursery Clo 10 B3

Oaklands Way 9 C3
Oakmead 9 D2
Old Barn Clo 12 B2
Old Hadlow Rd 10 B3
Old London Rd 9 D3
Orchard Dri 10 B2
Orchard Lea 8 B2

Park Av 9 C2
Park Villas 7 B1
Parkway 10 A2
Pembroke Rd 12 B2
Pembury Gro 13 C2
Pembury Rd 12 B2
Pen Way 10 B2
Pine Ridge 9 C2
Portland Clo 10 B1
Portman Pk 13 C1
Postern La 13 D2
Powder Mills 12 A1
Preston Rd 12 B2
Priestley Dri 10 B2
Priory Gro 12 B2
Priory Rd 12 B2
Priory St 12 B2
Priory Walk 12 B2

Quarry Gdns 12 B2
Quarry Hill Rd 12 B3
Quarry Rise 12 B3
Quincewood Gdns 9 D1

Raeburn Clo 10 B2
Rembrandt Clo 10 B2
Reynolds Clo 10 B2
Ridgeway Cres 10 A3
Riding La 8 B1
Ridings Pk 8 B1
Rings Hill 8 A2
River Lawn 12 B2
River Walk 13 C2
Riverside Ct 13 C2
Rochester Rd 10 A3
Rodney Av 10 B3
Romney Way 10 B3
Rose St 13 C2
Rother Rd 9 D2
Rowan Shaw 10 A2
Royal Av 13 C2
Royal West Kent Av 10 A3
Rutherford Way 10 A1

St Bernards Rd 9 D2
St Georges Mews 12 B2
St James Clo 10 B1
St Marys Rd 12 B3
St Pauls Clo 10 A2
St Stephens St 12 B2
Salisbury Rd 10 A3
Saville Clo 10 B1
School La 7 B3
Scott Rd 12 B3
Seabrook Rd 9 C3
Severn Clo 9 D2
Shakespeare Rd 12 B3
Shelton Clo 9 D2
Sheraton Park 7 B3

Shipbourne Rd 10 A3
Shrublands 13 C1
Silver Clo 12 B3
Silverhurst Dri 9 D2
Skinners Ter 12 B2
Smithers Clo 7 B1
Somerhill Rd 13 C2
Sovereign Clo 13 C2
Sovereign Way 13 C2
Springwell Rd 12 B3
Stacey Rd 9 C3
Stafford Rd 12 B1
Stainer Rd 10 B2
Stair Rd 10 B3
Steers Pl 7 A1
Stocks Green Rd 8 A2
Strawberry Vale 13 C2
Streamside 10 A2
Sullivan Rd 10 B2
Sussex Rd 12 B2
Swanland Dri 12 A3

Tainter Rd 7 A1
Tamar Rd 9 D2
Tannery Rd 13 C2
Tanyard Farm 10 B3
Thames Rd 9 D2
The Avenue 12 B1
The Birches 12 B3
The Brent 9 D2
The Cherry Orchard 7 A1
The Chase 9 D2
The Crescent 12 B1
The Drive 12 B3
The Freehold 7 A1
The Grove 13 C1
The Maltings 7 A2
The Paddock 7 A1
The Ridgeway 10 A3
The Slade 12 B1
The Spinney 12 B3
Thorpe Av 10 A2
Three Elm La 11 C2
Tilebarn Corner 10 B3
Toby Gdns 7 A2
Tonbridge By-Pass 7 A2
Tonbridge Rd 7 A2
Town Acres 9 D3
Tree Tops 12 B3
Trench Rd 9 D2
Truro Walk 10 A2
Tudeley La 13 C3
Tulip Tree Clo 12 B2
Turner Rd 10 B2
Tweed Rd 9 D2
Twyford Rd 7 A1
Tyne Rd 9 D2

Upper Haysden La 12 A3
Uridge Cres 9 D3
Uridge Rd 9 D3

Vale Rise 13 C2
Vale Rd 13 C2
Valley Forge Clo 10 B3
Vaughan Av 10 B2
Vauxhall Gdns 13 C3
Victoria Rd 7 B3

Walters Farm Rd 13 C2
Walton Rd 10 B2
Water Slippe 7 A1
Waterloo Pl 12 B2
Waterloo Rd 12 B2
Watts Cross Rd 8 A1
Waveney Rd 9 D2
Weald View Rd 12 B3
Wealdon Clo 8 B3
Welland Rd 9 D3
Wells Clo 10 A3
West Rise 12 B3
Wetton Clo 12 A3
Wheatsheaf Way 10 A2
Whistler Rd 10 A1
White Cottage Rd 10 A2
White Lake Rd 9 D2
Whiteoak Clo 10 A3
Willow Lea 9 D1
Wilson Clo 8 B2
Wilson Rd 10 B2
Winchester Rd 10 A3
Wincliffe Rd 12 B2
Woodfield Av 8 B2
Woodfield Rd 12 B2
Woodland Walk 10 B2
Woodlands Rd 12 B3
Woodside Rd 12 B3
Woodview Cres 8 B3
Wye Rd 9 D2

Yardley Clo 10 B3
Yardley Park Rd 10 A3
York Par 9 D2
York Rd 10 A2

TUNBRIDGE WELLS

Albany Hill 19 C2
Albert St 18 B2
Albion Rd 18 B2
Alders Clo 15 D3
All Saints Rd 18 B1
Allan Clo 17 C2
Allandale Rd 19 C1
Amberleaze Dri 21 C3

Amherst Rd 18 B2
Andrew Rd 15 D3
Andrews Clo 19 C2
Apple Tree La 19 C1
Apsley St 17 D3
Argyle Rd 15 C2
Arundel Rd 23 C2
Ashdown Clo 18 A3
Ashenden Walk 20 A2
Asher Reeds 16 B3
Ashley Gdns 17 C2
Ashley Park Clo 17 C2
Ashurst Pl 16 A3
Aspen Way 15 D3
Auckland Rd 18 B2
Avon St 18 B2

Banner Farm Rd 23 D2
Barden Rd 16 B1
Barnetts Way 15 D3
Barnfield 23 C3
Barrow ...a 16 B3
Basinghall St 18 B2
Batchelors 21 D2
Bayhall Rd 18 B3
Bayham Rd 23 C3
Beagles Wood Rd 21 D2
Bedford Rd 15 C3
Beech St 18 B2
Bel Gro 23 C2
Belfield Rd 21 C3
Belgrave Rd 18 B2
Beltring Rd 18 A2
Benhall Mill Rd 23 D3
Bentham Hill 14 B3
Berkeley Rd 23 C2
Beulah Rd 18 B2
Bidborough Ridge 14 B1
Birch Clo 19 C1
Birch Rd 19 C1
Birch Way 19 C1
Birchetts Av 16 B3
Birchwood Av 14 B2
Birken Rd 19 C1
Birling Dri 23 C2
Birling Park Rd 23 C3
Birling Rd 23 C3
Bishops Down Park Rd 18 A2
Bishops Down Rd 18 A3
Blackhurst La 20 A3
Blackthorn Av 15 D3
Blakeways 19 C1
Blatchington Rd 23 C2
Boundary 23 D2
Bounds Oak Way 14 B2
Bowen Rd 17 C2
Boyne Park 18 A2
Bracken Clo 19 C2
Bracken Rd 19 C2
Breedon Av 15 C3
Brendon Clo 19 C2
Bretland Rd 17 C2
Brian Cres 15 C3
Bright Ridge 14 B3
Broad Oak Clo 23 C2
Broadcroft 23 C3
Broadgrove 23 C3
Broadmead 22 B3
Broadmead Av 22 B3
Broadwater Ct 22 B3
Broadwater Down 22 B2
Broadwater La 22 B2
Broadwater Rise 22 C2
Brokes Way 15 C3
Brook Rd 19 C1
Brookhurst Gdns 14 B2
Brooklands 19 C1
Broom La 16 A3
Broom Park 16 A3
Broomhill Park Rd 14 B3
Broomhill Rd 17 D1
Brunswick Ter 23 C2
Buckingham Rd 23 C2
Bucklers Clo 18 B3
Bullingstone La 16 A1
Bulls Pl 21 C3
Burdett Rd 17 C3
Burnthouse La 16 B2
Burslem Rd 19 C1
Bushy Gill 16 B3
Byng Rd 18 A2

Cabbage Stalk La 22 B2
Cadogan Gdns 18 B3
Caley Rd 19 C1
Calverley Park 18 B3
Calverley Park Cres 18 B3
Calverley Park Gdns 18 B3
Calverley St 18 B3
Calverley St 18 B3
Cambrian Rd 18 B1
Cambridge Gdns 23 D2
Cambridge St 18 B3
Camden Av 21 C3
Camden Ct 21 C3
Camden Hill 23 D2
Camden Pk 23 D2
Camden Rd 18 B2
Campbell Rd 18 A2
Canterbury Rd 21 D3
Carlton Cres 18 B3
Carlton Rd 18 B3
Carvele Av 15 C3
Castle Rd,
Southborough 15 C2
Castle Rd, Tun Wells 18 A3
Castle St 23 C2
Catherine Pl 18 B3

Name	Ref
Cavendish Dri	23 D2
Cedar Ridge	19 C2
Chalket La	21 C3
Chandos Rd	18 B2
Chapman Way	15 D3
Charles St	15 C3
Charltons Way	22 B2
Chenies Clo	23 C3
Cherry Tree Rd	22 B2
Chester Av	19 C3
Chestnut Av	15 C3
Chestnut Clo	15 C3
Chieveley Dri	23 D2
Chilston Clo	18 B2
Chilston Rd	18 B2
Chiltern Walk	19 C2
Christ Church Av	23 C1
Church Rd, Pembury	21 C2
Church Rd, Southborough	14 B2
Church Rd, Tun Wells	18 A3
Clanricarde Gdns	18 B3
Clanricarde Rd	18 B3
Claremont Gdns	23 C2
Claremont Rd	23 C2
Clarence Rd	18 B3
Clarence Row	18 B3
Clarendon Rd	23 C2
Clarendon Way	23 C2
Cleeve Av	19 C3
Cleveland	19 C2
Clifton Pl	23 C2
Clifton Rd	19 C1
Clock House	19 D1
Coach Rd	17 C3
Cobbetts Ride	22 B2
Cobhams	16 B1
Colebrook Rd	18 B1
College Dri	19 C2
Colonels Way	15 C2
Commercial Rd	18 B2
Common View	17 C3
Concord Clo	19 C2
Coneyburrow Rd	19 C2
Coniston Av	17 D2
Connaught Way	18 A2
Constitution Hill Rd	14 B2
Cornford Clo	21 C3
Cornford La	19 D2
Court Rd	18 A2
Cranwell Rd	17 C2
Crescent Rd	19 C3
Cromwell Rd	14 B3
Crundwell Rd	18 A2
Culverden Av	18 A2
Culverden Down	18 A2
Culverden Park	18 A2
Culverden Park Rd	18 A2
Culverden Sq	18 B2
Culverden St	18 B2
Cumberland Walk	23 C2
Cunningham Rd	18 B1
Dale St	18 B2
Darnley Dri	14 B1
Delves Av	23 D2
Denbigh Rd	18 B1
Dene Way	16 B1
Derwent Dri	18 A2
Devonshire Dri	22 B3
Dillon Way	19 C1
Doone Brae	15 C2
Doric Av	15 C3
Doric Clo	14 B3
Dorking Rd	18 B2
Dornden Dri	16 B3
Dorset Rd	23 D2
Dower House Cres	14 B2
Draper St	15 C2
Dudley Rd	18 B2
Dukes Rd	18 B2
Dunstan Gro	18 B2
Dunstan Rd	18 B2
Dynevor Rd	18 B1
Earls Rd	18 A2
East Cliff Rd	18 B1
Eastlands Clo	22 B2
Eastlands Rd	22 B2
Eden Rd	23 C2
Edward St, Rusthall	17 C3
Edward St, Southborough	15 C3
Elm Rd	15 C3
Elmhurst Av	21 C2
Elphicks Pl	23 C3
Ely La	18 B2
Eridge Rd	22 B2
Erskine Park Rd	17 C2
Essex Clo	22 B3
Etherington Hill	14 A3
Ewhurst La	16 B1
Fairfield Rd	19 C2
Fairlight Clo	15 C2
Fairmile Rd	19 C2
Farmcombe Clo	23 C2
Farmcombe La	23 C2
Farmcombe Rd	23 C2
Farnham Clo	16 B3
Farnham La	16 B1
Ferbies	16 B1
Ferndale	18 B2
Ferndale Clo	18 B2
Ferndale Gdns	18 B2
Ferndale Rd	19 C2
Fernhurst Cres	15 C2
Fir Tree Rd	18 A3
First St	16 B3
Fordcombe Rd	16 A3
Forest Rd	23 D2
Forest View	21 C2
Forest Way, Hawkenbury	23 D2
Forest Way, Pembury	21 C2
Forge Rd	15 C3
Forstal	16 B3
Frankfield Rise	23 C2
Franks Hollow Rd	14 A2
Frant Rd	23 C2
Fremlin Clo	17 C2
Friars Way	19 C1
Friezland Rd	22 B2
Frog La	23 C2
Furnival Ct	22 B3
Garden Rd	18 B2
Garden St	18 B3
Garlinge Rd	15 C3
Gate Farm Rd	14 A1
Gibbetts	16 B3
Gimble Way	21 C2
Gipps Cross Rd	16 B3
Gladstone Rd	17 C3
Glebelands	14 A2
Glenmore Pk	22 B3
Golding St	18 B2
Goods Station Rd	18 B2
Gordon Rd	18 B1
Gorse Rd	19 C2
Grampion Clo	19 C2
Grange Gdns	17 D2
Grange Rd	17 D2
Granville Rd	18 B2
Great Bounds Dri	14 B2
Great Brooms Rd	15 D3
Great Courtland	16 B3
Great Footway	18 B3
Grecian Rd	23 C2
Greenfield Clo	17 C2
Greenleas	21 C3
Greenway	19 C1
Greggswood Rd	19 C1
Grendon Pk	15 C3
Groombridge Hill	19 A3
Grosvenor Bridge	18 B2
Grosvenor Pk	18 B2
Grosvenor Rd	18 B2
Grove Av	23 C2
Grove Hill Gdns	23 C2
Grove Hill Rd	23 C1
Grover St	18 B2
Guildford Rd	23 C1
Halls Hole Rd	19 C3
Hamilton Ct	18 B2
Hanover Rd	18 B2
Hardinge Av	14 B2
Harescroft	23 C3
Hargate Clo	22 B3
Harlands Way	14 B2
Harley Ct	18 A2
Harmony St	17 D3
Harries Rd	19 C1
Hasletts Clo	18 B2
Hastings Rd	21 C3
Hawkenbury Clo	23 D2
Hawkenbury Rd	23 D2
Hawthorn Walk	20 A2
Haysden La	14 A1
Hazelwood Clo	19 C1
Heathfields	19 C2
Henley Clo	19 C2
Henwood Green Rd	21 C2
Henwoods Cres	21 C3
Henwoods Mount	21 D3
Herons Way	21 D2
High Beeches	19 C2
High Brooms Rd	18 B1
High Gro	23 C3
High Rocks La	22 A2
High St, Bidborough	14 A2
High St, Pembury	21 C3
High St, Tun Wells	23 C2
High Woods La	19 C3
Highfield Clo	21 C3
Highfield Rd	18 B1
Hilbert Clo	19 C2
Hilbert Rd	19 C2
Hill Crest	15 C3
Hill Crest Dri	19 C1
Hill Garth	18 B1
Hill St	18 B2
Hill View Rd	17 C2
Hither Chantlers	16 B3
Holden Corner	14 B3
Holden Park Rd	15 C3
Holden Rd	14 B3
Hollin Clo	18 A2
Hollyshaw Clo	23 C2
Holmewood Ridge	16 B3
Holmewood Road	18 B1
Holmhurst Clo	18 A3
Home Farm La	20 A2
Homewood Rd	16 B3
Hope Ter	18 A2
Hopwood Gdns	18 B2
Horizon Clo	15 D3
Howard Gdns	23 C2
Humboldt Ct	19 C2
Hungershall Pk	18 A3
Hungershall Rd	22 B2
Hunters Way	22 B2
Hurstwood La	18 A3
Hythe Clo	15 C3
Impala Gdns	18 B1

INDUSTRIAL ESTATES

Name	Ref
Colebrook Ind. Est.	20 A1
Haslemere High Brooms Estate	15 D1
Kingstanding Business Park	20 A1
Spa Ind. Est	20 A2
Inner London Rd	18 A3
Ironstones	17 C3
John St	18 A2
Keel Gdns	14 B3
Kemble Clo	19 C1
Kendal Pk	17 D2
Kensington St	18 B2
Kent Rd	18 A2
Kibbles La	14 B3
King George V Hill	19 C2
Kings Toll	21 D3
Kingswood Clo	19 C3
Kingswood Rd	19 C3
Kirby Ct	18 B3
Kirkdale Rd	18 B2
Knights Clo	21 C2
Knights Pl	21 C2
Knights Ridge	21 C2
Knightsbridge Clo	18 A2
Knowle Clo	16 B3
Lady's Gift Rd	14 B3
Lake Rd	17 D3
Lamberts Rd	20 A2
Lambourn Way	23 D2
Lampington Row	16 A3
Langholme Rd	16 B3
Langton Ridge	17 C3
Langton Rd	17 C3
Lansdowne Rd	18 B3
Lansdowne Sq	18 B3
Laurel Bank	18 B1
Laurel Rd	19 C1
Laurel Way	19 C1
Leggs La	16 A2
Leicester Dri	22 B3
Leighton Clo	18 A1
Leneda Dri	22 B3
Lime Hill Rd	18 B3
Linden Clo	23 C2
Linden Gdns	23 C2
Linden Park Rd	23 C2
Link Way	19 C1
Lipscombe Rd	19 C2
Liptraps La	19 C1
Little Bounds Clo	14 B2
Little Footway	16 B3
Little Mount Sion	23 C2
London Rd, Southborough	14 B2
London Rd, Tun Wells	18 A3
Long Slip	16 B3
Long View Way	19 C1
Longfield Rd	20 A2
Longmeads	17 C3
Lonsdale Gdns	18 B3
Lower Green Rd, Pembury	21 C3
Lower Green Rd, Rusthall	17 C1
Madeira Pk	23 C2
Maidstone Rd	21 D1
Major Yorks Rd	18 A3
Malton Way	20 B3
Manor Clo	18 A3
Manor Pk	18 A3
Manor Rd, Rusthall	17 C2
Manor Rd, Southborough	14 B3
Maple Clo	23 C2
Market St, Hungershall Pk	23 C2
Market St, Tun Wells	18 B2
Marlborough Clo	17 D3
Maryland Rd	23 D2
Mayfield Rd	18 A2
Meadow Hill Rd	23 C1
Meadow Rd, Rusthall	17 C2
Meadow Rd, Southborough	15 C3
Meadow Rd, Tun Wells	18 B2
Mendip Walk	18 B2
Mercer St	18 B2
Mercers	16 B3
Mereworth Rd	18 B2
Merrion Clo	18 B1
Merrion Way	18 B2
Middle Walk	19 C1
Middlefield, Pembury	21 D2
Middlefield, Rusthall	17 C3
Milton Dri	19 C1
Moat Farm	23 C3
Molyneux Park	18 A2
Molyneux Park Gdns	18 A3
Monson Rd	18 B2
Montacute Gdns	23 C2
Montacute Rd	23 C2
Monteith Clo	16 B3
Montgomery Rd	18 B1
Mount Edgecombe Rd	18 A3
Mount Ephraim	18 A3
Mount Ephraim Rd	18 B3
Mount Pleasant Av	18 B3
Mount Pleasant Rd	18 B3
Mount Sion	23 C2
Mountfield Gdns	18 B3
Mountfield Rd	18 B3
Napier Rd	23 D2
Nellington Rd	17 C2
Nelson Rd	23 D2
Nevill Ct	17 D4
Nevill Gate	23 C2
Nevill Park	22 B1
Nevill St	23 C1
Nevill Ter	23 C2
New Camden Pk	23 D2
New England Rd	18 B1
Newcomen Rd	18 B2
Newlands Rise	18 B1
Newlands Road	18 B1
Newlands Way	18 B1
Newton Rd	18 B1
Norfolk Rd	23 C2
Norman Rd	18 B2
Norstead Gdns	18 B1
North Farm La	19 C1
North St	18 B3
Northfield Rd	16 B1
Norton Rd	15 C3
Nottidge Rd	22 B2
Nursery Rd	18 B1
Oak End Clo	15 C2
Oak Rd	19 C1
Oak Tree Clo	23 C2
Oakdale Rd	18 A2
Oakfield Court Rd	18 B3
Oakwood Rise	18 B1
Old Church Rd	21 C1
Old Gardens Clo	23 C3
Old House La	16 A2
Orchard Clo	19 C1
Orchidhurst	19 C1
Ox Lea	16 B3
Paddock Clo	21 C3
Park House Gdns	15 C2
Park Rd, Southborough	15 C2
Park Rd, Tun Wells	18 B2
Park St	18 B3
Parkwood Clo	19 C1
Parsonage Rd	17 C2
Parsonage Rd	17 C2
Pembury Clo	21 C2
Pembury Grange	19 D1
Pembury Hall Rd	21 C1
Pembury Rd	19 D2
Pembury Walks	20 B1
Pennine Walk	19 C2
Pennington Pl	15 C2
Pennington Rd	15 C2
Penshurst Rd, Bidborough	14 A2
Penshurst Rd, Speldhurst	16 B1
Petersfield	21 D2
Pinewood Gdns	15 C3
Pinewood Rd	19 C2
Polesden Rd	23 D2
Poona Rd	23 C2
Powdermill Clo	15 D3
Powdermill La	18 B1
Princes St	18 B3
Prospect Park	14 B2
Prospect Rd, Southborough	15 C3
Prospect Rd, Tun Wells	18 B3
Quarry Rd	18 B2
Queens Rd	18 B2
Ramslye Rd	22 B2
Rankine Rd	19 C1
Ravenswood Av	19 C2
Rectory Clo	14 A2
Red Leaf Clo	19 C1
Redwings La	21 C1
Reynolds La	18 A1
Richardson Rd	18 B2
Riddlesdale Av	18 B1
Ridgelands	14 A2
Ridgeway	21 C2
Rochdale Rd	18 B2
Rock Villa Rd	18 B2
Rockley Clo	19 C3
Rodmell Rd	23 C2
Roedean Rd	23 C2
Romford Rd	21 D2
Roopers	16 B1
Ropers Gate	22 B2
Rose Hill Walk	18 A3
Rossdale	19 C2
Roundhill Rd	23 D2
Rowan Tree Rd	22 B2
Rowans	21 D3
Royal Chase	18 A2
Ruscombe Clo	14 B2
Rushetts	16 B3
Rusthall High St	17 C2
Rusthall Pk	17 D3
Rusthall Rd	17 C3
Rustwick	17 D3
Rydal Clo	17 D2
Rydal Dri	17 D2
Rymers Clo	19 C1
St Andrews Park Rd	15 C3
St Davids Rd	18 B1
St Georges Pk	23 C3
St James Rd	18 B2
St James's Pk	18 B2
St John's Rd	18 B1
St Johns Park	15 C3
St Lawrence Av	14 B2
St Lukes Rd	18 B1
St Marks Rd	22 B3
St Marys La	16 B1
St Michaels Rd	18 B1
St Pauls St	17 C3
St Peter St	18 B3
Salisbury Rd, High Brooms	15 D3
Salisbury Rd, Langton Green	16 B3
Salisbury Rd, Rusthall	17 C2
Salomans Rd	17 C2
Sandhurst Av	21 D3
Sandhurst Clo	19 C1
Sandhurst Pk	19 C1
Sandhurst Rd	19 C1
Sandown Clo	20 A3
Sandown Gro	20 A3
Sandown Pk	20 A3
Sandrock Rd	19 C2
Saunders Rd	22 B2
Scotts Way	22 B3
Shaftesbury Rd	18 B2
Shandon Clo	18 B3
Sheffield Rd	15 C2
Shepherds Walk	19 C3
Sherbourne Clo	23 D2
Sherwood Way	19 C2
Shirley Gdns	17 C2
Shirley Gro	17 C2
Showfields Rd	22 B2
Shrubland Ct	19 C3
Sidney Clo	22 B3
Silverdale La	18 B1
Silverdale Rd	18 B1
Silwood Clo	19 C1
Sir Davids Pk	14 B3
Smythe Clo	14 B2
Snipe Clo	21 D2
Somerset Rd	18 B2
Somerville Gdns	18 A3
South Gro	23 C2
South View Rd	18 B1
Southfield Rd, Speldhurst	16 B1
Southfield Rd, Tun Wells	18 A1
Southfields Way	18 B1
Southwood Av	18 B2
Southwood Rd	17 C2
Speldhurst Hill	17 C1
Speldhurst Rd, Southborough	14 B3
Speldhurst Rd, Speldhurst	16 B2
Spring Cotts	17 C3
Spring Gdns	17 C3
Spring La	14 A2
Springfield Rd	15 C3
Springhead	19 C2
Squirrel Way	19 C2
Stafford Clo	19 D2
Stag Rd	20 A2
Stanam Rd	21 D3
Standen St	18 A2
Stanhope Rd	18 B2
Stanley Rd	18 B2
Stephens Rd	18 B2
Stewart Rd	18 B1
Stockland Green Rd	14 A3
Stone St	18 B2
Stonecourt La	21 D2
Stonewall Park Rd	16 B3
Stratford St	18 B2
Strawberry Clo	22 B3
Stuart Clo	22 B3
Summerhill Av	14 B3
Summervale Rd	22 B2
Sunhill Ct	21 C3
Sunnyside Rd	17 C3
Surrey Clo	22 B3
Sussex Clo	23 D2
Sutherland Rd	23 C1
Swallow Dri	20 B3
Sweepshill Clo	21 C2
Talbot Clo	19 C2
Taylor St	15 C3
Tea Garden La	22 A2
Tedder Rd	18 B1
The Boundary	17 C3
The Chase	18 B3
The Coppice	21 C2
The Crescent	14 B1
The Crossway	22 B2
The Fairways	18 B1
The Ferns	18 B3
The Forstal	21 D2
The Gill	21 D2
The Glebe, Bidborough	14 A2
The Glebe, Pembury	21 C2
The Grange	17 D3
The Grove	21 C2
The Hurst	19 C1
The Meadow	21 D2
The Meads	23 D2
The Midway	22 A2
The Paddock	21 C3
The Pantiles	23 C2
The Ridgeway	15 C3
The Ridings	19 D2
The Shaw	23 D2
The Spurway	22 A2
The Woodlands	21 D2
Theodore Clo	19 C1
Third St	16 B3
Thirlmere Rd	17 D2
Thomas St	18 A2
Thornfield Gdns	19 D2
Tonbridge Rd	20 B2
Trinity St	19 C3
Tristan Gdns	17 C2

Tudor Ct 22 B2
Tunnel Rd 18 B2
Tuxford Rd 17 C2

Upper Cumberland
Walk 23 C2
Upper Dunstan Rd 18 B2
Upper Grosvenor Rd 18 B2
Upper Nellington 17 C3
Upper Profit 16 B3
Upper Stephens 18 B3
Upper St 17 D3
Upton Quarry 16 B3

Vale Av, Southborough 15 C3
Vale Av, Tun Wells 18 B3
Vale Rd, Southborough 15 C2
Vale Rd, Tun Wells 23 C1
Valley Rd 17 C2
Valley View 15 C2
Varney St 18 B2
Vauxhall La 15 D1
Vermont Rd 17 C3
Vernon Rd 18 B2
Vicarage Rd 15 C2
Victoria Rd,
Southborough 14 B2
Victoria Rd, Tun Wells 18 B2

Wallace Clo 23 C3
Wallers 17 C1
Warwick Pk 23 C2
Warwick Rd 23 C2
Waterdown Rd 22 B2
Waterfield 23 C3
Waverley Dri 19 D1
Weare Rd 15 D3
Welbeck Av 15 D3
Weller Rd 17 C2
West Park Av 15 C3
Westbrook Ter 23 D2
Western Rd,
Southborough 15 C3
Western Rd, Tun Wells 18 B2
Westway 21 C2
Westwood Rd 17 C2
Whitefield Rd 18 A2
Whybourne Cres 23 D2
Wickham Gdns 17 C2
William St 18 A2
Willow Tree Rd 22 B2
Willow Walk 19 C1
Wilman Rd 18 B1
Wiltshire Rd 19 C1
Windmill St 18 B3
Winstone Scott Av 16 A3
Wolseley Rd 18 B1
Wood St 18 B2
Woodbury Park Gdns 18 B2
Woodbury Park Rd 18 B2
Woodhill Pk 21 C3
Woodland Rd 18 B1
Woodland Way 14 A2
Woodlands Clo 18 B3
Woodsgate Way 21 C3
Woodside Clo 21 D3
Woodside Rd, Pembury 21 D3
Woodside Rd, Rusthall 17 D2
Wooley Clo 14 B3
Wooley Rd 14 B3
Wybourn Rise 23 D3

Yew Tree Rd 15 C3
York Rd 18 B3

CRANBROOK
Angley Rd 6 A2
Angley Walk 6 B1
Bakers Cross 6 B2
Bank St 6 A2
Bramley Dri 6 B3
Brickenden Dri 6 B3
Brickenden Rd 6 B2
Brookside 6 B2
Carriers Rd 6 B2
Causton Rd 6 A2
Dorothy Av 6 B3
Frythe Clo 6 B3
Frythe Cres 6 B3
Frythe Walk 6 B3
Frythe Way 6 B3
Goddards Clo 6 A3
Golford Rd 6 B2
Goudhurst Rd 6 B1
Greenway 6 A2
Handley Dri 6 A2
Hawkhurst Rd 6 A3
High St 6 B2
Hopes Dri 6 B2
Hopes Rd 6 B2
Jockey La 6 B2
Kirby Clo 6 B3
New Rd 6 A2
Oatfield Clo 6 A2
Oatfield Dri 6 A2
Orchard Way 6 A3
Quakers Dri 6 B1
Quakers La 6 B1
Rope Walk 6 B2
St Dunstans Walk 6 B2
Sheafe Dri 6 A2
Stone St 6 B2
Swifts Vw 6 B1
The Hill 6 B2
The Tanyard 6 B2
Turner Av 6 B3
Waterloo Rd 6 B2
Wheatfield Clo 6 A2

Wheatfield Dri 6 A2
Wheatfield Lea 6 A2
Wheatfield Way 6 A2
Willesley Gdns 6 B1

CROWBOROUGH
Alderbrook Clo 26 A2
Alderbrook Way 26 A2
Aldervale Cotts 26 A2
Alice Bright La 26 A1
Aviemore Rd 24 A2
Badgers Clo 24 B2
Barnfield 25 C2
Beacon Clo 24 B2
Beacon Gdns 24 B2
Beacon Rd 24 A3
Beacon Rd West 24 B2
Beaconwood 24 B2
Beaver Clo 25 C3
Beeches Farm Rd 25 C3
Beeches Rd 25 C2
Belvedere Gdns 25 C3
Bentley Path 24 B2
Birches Clo 24 B1
Blackness Rd 25 C3
Blacknest 25 C3
Booker Clo 25 C3
Bracken Clo 25 D3
Bridge Dri 25 C2
Bridger Way 24 B2
Brincliffe 24 B2
Broadway 25 D3
Brook Clo 24 A1
Brook Ter 24 A1
Brook View 24 A1
Brooklands Av 26 B1
Bryant Fields 24 B2
Buller Clo 26 B2
Burdett Rd 25 D3
Charity Farm Way 24 B2
Chequers Clo 25 C2
Chequers Way 25 C2
Church Rd 24 B2
Clackhams La 26 B3
Clifford Ct 24 B3
Coldharbour Clo 24 B3
Coldharbour Cotts 24 B3
Combe End Rd 24 B1
Common Wood Rise 24 B1
Coopers La 24 A1
Coopers Wood 24 A1
Cornford Clo 24 B3
Croft Rd 24 B2
Croham Rd 24 B2
Crowborough Hill 25 C3
Dodds Hill 25 C2
East Beeches Rd 25 C2
Elm Court Cotts 24 B1
Eridge Gdns 25 C2
Eridge Rd 24 B2
Fairview La 24 B1
Farningham Rd 25 D3
Fermor Rd 26 B1
Fermor Row 24 B3
Fermor Way 24 B3
Fielden La 24 A3
Fielden Rd 24 A2
Figg La 24 B3
Forest Dene 25 D3
Forest Pk 24 A2
Forest Rise 25 D3
Furnace Mead 24 A2
Ghyll Rd 24 B1
Gilridge Grn 24 B1
Gladstone Rd 24 B3
Glenmore Rd 24 A2
Glenmore Rd East 24 A2
Goldsmith Av 24 B2
Gordon Rd 24 B2
Graycotts Dri 24 B1
Green La 25 C2
Harecombe Rise 24 B3
Harecombe Road 24 B3
Harlequin La 24 B3
Heather Walk 25 D3
Heavegate Rd 24 A2
Herne Down 26 B1
Herne Rd 24 B3
High Broom La 26 A1
High Broom Rd 26 B1
High Cross Flds 24 B2
High Rise 24 B3
High St 24 B2
Highlands Clo 24 B3
Hilders Farm Clo 25 C3
Hill Clo 24 B2
Hill Rise 25 C2
Hoadleys La 24 A3
Hookswood Rd 24 C2
Huntingdon Rd 24 B3
Hurtis Hill 26 B1
Hydehurst Clo 24 B3
INDUSTRIAL ESTATES:
Lexden Lodge
Ind. Est. 25 D3
Inhams Wood 24 B1
Jefferies Way 24 B1
Kemps Farm Rd 25 C3
Kings Chase 24 B2
Kings Court 24 B2
Knowle Clo 26 B3
Links Clo 24 A3
Little Sunnyside 24 B3
London Rd 24 B1
Lordswell La 24 B1
Lower Saxonbury 24 B2
Loxfields Gdns 25 C3
Luxford Dri 26 B2
Luxford La 26 B2

Luxford Rd 26 B2
Manor Way 24 B3
Mardens Hill 24 A1
Medway 25 C3
Melfort Rd 24 A3
Mill Cres 24 B2
Mill Dri 24 B2
Mill La 24 B2
Millbrook Rd 25 C2
Moffins Hill 26 B3
Montargis Way 24 B3
Mount Pleasant 26 B3
Myrtle Rd 24 B3
Nevill Rd 24 B2
New Rd 24 B2
Norbury Clo 24 B1
North Beeches Rd 25 C3
Oakhurst Dri 25 C2
Ocklye Rd 24 A2
Old La, Blacknest 25 C3
Old La, St. Johns 24 A2
Oliver Clo 25 C3
Osborne Hill 25 C3
Osborne Rd 25 C3
Palesgate 25 C2
Park Cres 24 B2
Park La 24 B2
Park Rd 24 B2
Pilmer Rd 24 B2
Pine Gro 24 B1
Pleasant View Rd 24 B2
Pound La 25 C2
Poundfield Rd 25 C2
Protts Folly La 24 B3
Queens Rd 24 B3
Rannoch Rd West 24 A2
Rannoch Rd 24 A2
Rochester Way 25 C3
Rockingham Way 26 B2
Rose Cotts 24 B2
Rother Clo 26 B2
Rotherfield Rd 26 B3
Rotherhill Rd 26 B2
St Johns Rd 24 A1
St Michaels La 26 B2
St Richards Way 26 B2
Sandridge 24 B3
Saxonbury Clo 24 B2
School La 24 B3
School La, St. Johns 24 A1
Sefton Chase 25 C2
Sefton Way 25 C2
Shaw Field 25 C3
Sheep Plain 24 A3
Sheiling Rd 24 B2
Shepherds Walk 25 C3
Simons Clo 25 C3
Smugglers La 24 A1
South St 24 B3
Southridge Rd 24 B3
Southview Clo 24 B3
Southview Rd 24 B3
Springfield Clo 25 C2
Springfield Way 24 B3
Station Rd 25 D3
Stone Cross Rd 26 A1
Swift Clo 24 A3
Sybron Way 25 D3
Tanner Way 25 C3
The Close 24 B2
The Martlets 24 B3
The Meadows 24 B3
The Park 24 B2
The Twitten 24 B3
Tollwood Pk 25 C3
Tollwood Rd 25 C3
Treblers Rd 26 B3
Trenches Rd 24 B3
Troy Clo 26 B3
Tubwell La 26 B3
Valley Rd 24 B2
Victoria Rd 25 D3
Wallis Clo 26 B2
Walshes Rd 26 A2
Warren Gdns 24 B2
Warren Rd 24 B2
Waylands Av 26 B1
Wealden Clo 24 B2
Wellesley Clo 24 A3
West Beeches Rd 25 C3
West Way 24 B1
Western Gdns 26 B3
Western Rd 26 B3
White Hill Clo 24 B3
Whitehill Rd 24 B3
Willowmead 26 B1
Wincroft Rd 24 A2
Windsor Pl 25 C3
Windsor Rd 25 D3
Wolfe Clo 25 C3
Woodland Way 26 B1
Woodside 24 B2

EDENBRIDGE
Albion Way 4 A1
Ashcombe Dri 4 A1
Barnhawe 4 A2
Briar Clo 4 B2
Cedar Dri 4 A2
Chestnut Clo 4 A2
Church Field 4 B3
Church St 4 B3
Clover Walk 4 B2
Coomb Field 4 A3
Croft La 4 B2
Crouch House Rd 4 A2
Crown Rd 4 B1
Enterprise Way 4 A2
Fairmead Rd 4 A1

Farmstead Dri 4 B2
Field Rd 4 B2
Fircroft Way 4 A2
Forge Croft 4 B3
Four Elms Rd 4 A2
Foxglove Clo 4 B2
Frant Field 4 B3
Grange Clo 4 B2
Great Mead 4 A2
Greenfield 4 B3
Harrow Clo 4 B3
Hawthorn Clo 4 A2
Heron Clo 4 B2
Hever Rd 4 B2
High Fields 4 A1
High St 4 A2
Hilders Clo 4 A1
Hilders La 4 A1
Hillcrest Rd 4 A1
Homestead Rd 4 A1
Hopgarden Clo 4 B2
INDUSTRIAL ESTATES:
Enterprise Way
Ind. Est 4 A1
Fircroft Way Ind. Est.
Hever Rd Ind. Est. 4 B3
Katherine Rd 4 B3
Kestrel Clo 4 B2
Leathermarket 4 B3
Lingfield Rd 4 A3
Lucilina Dri 4 A3
Lynmead Clo 4 A3
Magpie Green 4 B2
Main Rd 4 A1
Mallard Way 4 B2
Manor House Gdns 4 A3
Manor Rd 4 A3
Marl Hurst 4 A1
Marlpit Clo 4 A1
Meadow La 4 A1
New House Ter 4 A2
Oakfield Rd 4 A1
Orchard Clo 4 A2
Orchard Dri 4 A2
Oxfield 4 B2
Park Av 4 A2
Park View Clo 4 A2
Penlee Clo 4 A2
Pine Gro 4 A2
Pit La 4 A1
Plough Walk 4 B2
Plover Clo 4 B2
Queens Ct 4 B3
Ridge Way 4 B1
Riverside Ct 4 B3
Riverside 4 B3
Robyns Way 4 B3
Rowfield 4 B2
Skeynes Pk 4 A3
Skeynes Rd 4 A3
Skinners La 4 B2
Smithyfield 4 B2
Sorrell Clo 4 B2
Speedwell Clo 4 B2
Springfield Rd 4 A2
Stackfield 4 B2
Stanbridge Rd 4 A2
Stangrove Rd 4 A2
Station App 4 A2
Station Rd 4 A2
Stonefield 4 B2
Streat Field 4 B3
Swan La 4 A2
Swan Ridge 4 B1
The Brownings 4 A1
The Limes 4 A3
The Plat 4 B3
The Square 4 B3
Victoria Clo 4 B3
Victoria Rd 4 B3
Wainhouse Clo 4 B2
Water Lakes 4 B3
Wayside Dri 4 B2
Westways 4 A2
Woodland Dri 4 A2
Woodpecker Clo 4 B2

PADDOCK WOOD
Alders Cotts 28 A3
Alders Rd 28 A3
Allington Rd 29 C2
Ashcroft Rd 29 C3
Badsell Rd 28 B2
Ballard Way 29 C2
Birch Rd 29 C2
Bowls Pl 29 C2
Bramley Gdns 29 C2
Bullion Clo 29 C2
Catts Pl 29 D3
Chantlers Hill 29 C3
Church La 28 A3
Church Rd 29 C2
Claverdell Rd 29 C2
Cobbs Clo 29 C2
Cogate Rd 29 C2
Colts Hill 28 A3
Commercial Rd 29 C2
Concord Clo 29 C2
Crittenden La 28 A3
Dimmock Clo 29 C2
Eastwell Clo 29 C2
Eldon Way 29 C2
Falmouth Pl 28 A2
Five Oak Green Rd 28 A2
Forest Rd 29 C2
Fuggles Clo 29 C3
Goldings 29 C3

Granary 29 D2
Haywain Clo 29 C3
Hop Pocket La 29 C2
Hornbeam Clo 29 C3
INDUSTRIAL ESTATES:
Eldon Ind. Est 29 C2
Paddock Wood
Distribution Centre 29 D2
Transfesa 29 D2
Kent Clo 29 C2
Keyworth Clo 29 C2
Larch Gro 29 C2
Larkfield 28 A2
Laxton Gdns 29 C2
Le Temple Rd 29 D2
Linden Clo 29 C3
Lucknow Rd 29 C2
Lucks La 29 C1
Macdonald Ct 29 C2
Maidstone Rd,
Five Oak Green 28 B2
Maidstone Rd,
Paddock Wood 29 C3
Mascalls Court Rd 29 C3
Mascalls Park 29 C2
Mercers Clo 29 C2
Mile Oak Rd 29 D3
Mount Pleasant 29 D3
New Rd 29 C2
Newton Gdns 29 C2
North Down Clo 29 C2
Nortons Way 28 A2
Nursery Rd 29 C2
Oak Rd 28 A2
Oaklea Rd 29 C3
Old Kent Rd 29 C2
Pearsons Green Rd 29 D3
Pemble Clo 28 A2
Pinewood Clo 29 C2
Queen St 29 D3
Ribston Gdns 29 C2
Ringden Av 29 C3
St Andrews Clo 29 C2
St Andrews Rd 29 C2
Station App 29 C2
Station Rd 29 C2
Sycamore Gdns 29 C3
Sychem La 28 A2
Sychem Pl 28 A2
The Bines 29 C3
The Forge 28 A2
The Greenways 29 C3
Tolhurst Rd 28 A2
Tutsham Way 29 C2
Wagon La 29 D1
Walnut Clo 29 C2
Warrington Rd 29 C2
Whitstead Rd 28 A2
Willow Cres 28 A2
Woodlands 29 C2
Yeoman Gdns 29 C2

WADHURST
Balaclava La 5 B1
Bankside 5 A2
Bayham Ct 5 A2
Blacksmith La 5 B3
Brinkers La 5 B3
Castle Walk 5 A2
Cockmount La 5 A2
Courthope Av 5 B3
Crittles Ct 5 B3
Deepdene 5 B2
George St 5 B2
Gloucester Rd 5 A2
Green Sq 5 A2
High St 5 B2
Highbury Pl 5 B2
Hollydene Rd 5 B2
Holmsdale Clo 5 A2
INDUSTRIAL ESTATES:
Durgates Ind. Est 5 A2
Jonas Dri 5 A2
Jonas La 5 A2
Lamberhurst Rd 5 B2
Mayfield La 5 A3
Mayfield Pk 5 A2
Mount Pleasant 5 A2
Old Station Rd 5 A1
Osmers Hill 5 B1
Pell Clo 5 B2
Queens Cotts 5 B3
Snape View 5 B3
South View Rd 5 A2
Southfields 5 A2
Sparrows Grn 5 A2
Station Rd 5 A2
Stonebridge La 5 A1
Stonecross Rd 5 B3
Tapsells La 5 A2
The Leas 5 B1
The Marlpit 5 A2
The Square 5 A2
Three Oaks La 5 A1
Townlands Rd 5 B3
Turners Green La 5 B1
Turners Green Rd 5 B1
Washwell La 5 B3
Waters Cotts 5 B3
Watts Clo 5 B3
Weald View 5 B2
Wellington Pl 5 A2
Western Rd 5 A2
Whitegate La 5 A1
Windmill La 5 A3
Wyck La 5 B1